Rhythm And Poetry

Mr.MadLove's R.A.P.

Terrence Williams

BookLeaf
Publishing

India | USA | UK

Made with ❤ on the BookLeaf Publishing Platform
www.bookleafpub.in
www.bookleafpub.com

Dedication

To anyone who reads this book, thank you for showing some MadLove.

Preface

Music and poetry have always been two sides of the same rhythm—the heartbeat of expression, the language of the soul. *Rhythm And Poetry* is more than just an EP; it's a story told through lyrics, a journey through emotion, experience, and truth.

This book is a reflection of that journey. These lyrics, once carried by melodies and beats, now stand alone on the page, allowing every word, every line, to speak in its purest poetry form. Whether you've heard these songs before or are reading them for the first time, I hope they resonate with you, inspire you, and remind you of the power of words.

Welcome to *Rhythm And Poetry.*

Acknowledgements

Creating *Rhythm And Poetry* has been an incredible journey, and I couldn't have done it alone.

First and foremost, I want to thank my family and friends for their unwavering support, MadLove, and belief in my vision. Your encouragement has been the foundation that keeps me pushing forward.

To my community—your energy, passion, and connection to my words mean everything. You inspire me to keep writing, to keep creating, and to keep sharing my truth. This book is just as much yours as it is mine.

A huge thank you to the producers, engineers, song writers and creatives who helped bring my lyrics to life through sound. Your talent and dedication elevated this project beyond what I could have imagined.

Lastly, to everyone who has ever listened, read, or felt something from my words—thank you. Your support fuels my art, and I am forever grateful.

With MadLove and gratitude,

Tee Williams

1. Pressure Intro

You gotta be pure with your words

Don't always take everything so personally

It's best, just to stop assuming

And last but definitely not least

Always , by any means necessary

Go hard

2. Pressure Verse 1

When the Pressure on you
Tell me what you gonna do
Truth it come out
When your back against the wall
Times when in need
Heartbeat a speedball
Fall hell nah
Did my dirt and I never caught
So I thought
Karma, Universe's energy
I transformed it
Organic currency
Night terrors haunting me
In broad daylight
Appetite for destruction
Of goals that I write
Tint 5% , RV Mercedes
Family overseas quarterly vacation
Don't talk when angry
Don't Make decisions when sad

Don't promise when happy
And don't bring ish' to my pad
Songs and videos, sold out shows
Precise business plan
Madlove round' the globe
France to UK, London to Canada
Africa to Nasty, P'cola to Atlanta
Major milestone making a Billy
Rocking Coachella
With the crowd getting Litty
Voooo-Dooo, running from my magic
Mr. MadLove, DNA stay at it
4x4s that's known to hush the static
The impact will flip ya back like acrobatic
Practice and go harder
Believe in the process
Walk it like ya talk it
Hitting bottom of the nets

3. Pressure Hook

Put the slide in ya glide

Speak it into existence

Wanna stand out

Mite as well be different

Put the slide in ya glide

Speak it into existence

Wanna stand out

Mite as well be different

Put the glide

In ya' slide

Take a chance

Build ya life
5

4. Pressure Verse 2

Me and faith took a leap
Cannon ball out the plane
Nuts hang, spread wangs
Flew away from the same
Haters friends n' hoz
Strike a pose
At Arise, Bumbershoot
Crowd surf North Coast
Ski mask black gloves
Coming through the window
Of 'ya Church, Synagogue
Ya Mosque and ya' Temple
Can't unring a bell
So ring it with some facts
Man it sucks being judged
White, yellow, brown and black
Bucking through bars
Kill the lights drive slow
Cock the hammer back
Aye, aye, aye there they go

Aiming for the racist
The ped-a-phillios
The government too
I'm the New Negro
Intelligent man, Nubian can
Turn pain into power
Avatar of the land
No enemy within
One without can do no harm
I'm handsome as a mug
Kill him with the charm
Garage downstairs, pool is too
Homies come through
Full court alley-oop
Bank account like a phone number
Long distance
Recipe the music
And the studio the kitchen
Prayer hands open
Catching all the blessings
Filling me up, my grand-momma's dressing
Waking up to the sounds gulf of Mexico
Probably heard before I'm the New Negro

5. Let Me Sell It To Ya' Hook

Let me sell it to ya', What you got pimpin

Paint a perfect picture how to maximize figgas

Let me sell it to ya', Gone tell me den'

Game sold not told, Can ya' smell me pimpin

6. Let Me Sell It To Ya' Verse

1

You need game brotha man
Then let me sell it to ya
Cuz I can show ya' much better
Than I can tell it to ya
If you can't see it
Then you'll never feel it
And if ya' don't be it,
Then it was never real
Put some paper on it,
Do what it do homie
You keep it smooooth
Don't be a creeper homie
40 on my hip
And one bigger in the trunk
Sawed Off by my bed
Fa' all these crazy punks
Don't be fake man
Cuz the fake they get none
But when ya' stay real

Then real, yea you get some
Now get ya bread up
Chef Curry in the clutch
We Make and break rules
And we don't really give aaaaa
Now make a move on it,
Be bout ya biz cronie
Vibe out ride on cruise
While she chooses To do ,
Whatever makes me happy
So happy

7. Let Me Sell It To Ya' Verse

2

We ride I-10 and then we hit 95
Selling merch making ends
And we rock it live
Feel like Johnny 5
I am alive
Dazed and confused
Alright, alright, alright
Man it's really hot
Whipping in the kitchen'
Man I'm really hot
Merk ya' when I'm spittin'
Drinking alcohol to the last call
Baby ball but don't fall
Know your worth, don't get lost
Beastin, like ya got bad intentions
Im beastin, I'm beastin,
Hustle every weekend
Seeping deep like hollow point tips
Riding in my whip

With my Queen on my tip
I'm so fresh, so clean
Own properties where they greet me like a king
I flow good so ya' gotta pay me, yeah
Gather up my licks, yea ya gotta pay me

8. Let Me Sell It To Ya' Verse

3

I'm a boss coach,
Call me a cut throat
Follow the leader, Paid in full
Man I ain't no joke
Famaleez lust me,
They see me riding clean
Bend the block, watch em' jock
Like the police
Keep my grind tight
Praying keep my mind rite
It's going down
Glass Joe in a Tyson fight
Keep my fam close
I ain't got alotta friends
All money in mane'
MadLove and kin
My words and my balls,
Rebel with a cause
Easy math buy it all

Dave make the call
We Supply they demand
Product for the low low
Break em off
And we getting every cent worth
Now let me sell it to ya,
Not gone tell it to ya
If you aint showed MadLove
Behind my back
And I showed MadLove for a fact
Then ain't now way
That I'm a kick it wit ya
But let me sell it to ya

9. Be Free Intro

God put us in this
Game of Life
To play
But remember,
You are a General
And you must
Know the score at all times
Becuase the day shall come
When you must
Call your own plays
Living with MadLove
Is being Free

10. Be Free Verse 1

Family, friends, drugs, love and sex
All give pleasure today
And give pain the next
Became aware of my emotions
Then peace started to flourish
Past in the past
Now is the purpose
Was an Addict to my lover
Love another drug
Use a person to cover up pain
Then Both suffer
White flag to what it is
Married to one life
One day at a time
One beat and one mic
Drunk in denial
Judging outta jealousy
Stop Comparing myself to others
Let it get the best of me
A man can not survive Off

the bread alone
1 house 1 woman and man
Made a home

11. Be Free Hook

Be free

Tired of your job

Be free

Don't wanna go to college

Be free

Depression and anxiety

Tell me what it's gonna be

Be free

Lost and alone

Be free

Ya' hate it at home

Be free

Don't blow out ya' dome

Fall into a zone

Then ya' turn it on!

Be free

12. Be Free Verse 2

Adolescence habits
Made big girl choices
Prayed for faith
But listened
2 the Devil's voices
You heard it before
Hurt people, they hurt people
But ones raised with MadLove
Share MadLove equal
Possessions, materials
Money, power, respect
Connected with the wealthy
Big social status
The more you get
Does it make you more complete
Cars, Houses, jewelry is victory?
Happiness, a short-lived pleasure
My mind is on the joy
Cause' the joy live forever
Waiting on someone

To make meaning of your world ?
Another marriage
Or have another boy or a girl

13. Be Free Verse 3

Still Incomplete
Any moment u could snap
Don't wanna talk or hug
Keep ya' distance and ya' dap
Live dreams then expire
Or work then retire
Imagination lit
So I'm always gone be higher
Only getting stronger
Watch me as I grow
Bread keep it baking
Invest most my dough
Happy in my space
29 month seven
At home what a blessing
In the present I'm in heaven
Be free

14. Holding On Hook

Sometimes I

Disagree with

What I've become

But there's

No looking back

To what I've done

This means

Keep on moving

And keep holding on

I'm holding on and on

15. Holding On Verse 1

Take it back to a time
where he always had a dime
roll up on the scene
pimp caddy that shine
life goes on
as people move on
Gotta get it while I can
cause I'm already grown
The next man will
ain't no Time to kill
I feel living it up
how you keep it real
soon y'all gonna hear me
compare me
to Jay-Z, Nas, Pac
or Public Enemy
or it all could be
another dream
another night
or just another day

another felony ya' disappear
at least in time
We see it's gonna be OK
rekindle what's needed
make some new homey's
ones with MadLove
squash those phonies
they don't think
Ride dirty can't hold their drink
Massa's plan
way too many sink

16. Holding On Verse 1.5

Hella combo broke and depressed
With traits of violence
How to kill stress
Switch my appearance
My address
Same earth and birth
But mind had to rest
15 banging, 13 slanging, 11 training
Losing not gaining
The Moon's imagination blows
Angel's tears cover crown
When Universe raining
Religion and laws
Whites and blacks
Hoods and gangs
Sororities and frats
Plus Republicans and Democrats
What if one label
Like one mother
Raceless society

Sisters and brothers
Everybody in burbs
Nobody in the gutter
No worries
It's all gone to be tight
And let nothing block
The vision of my light

17. Holding On Verse 2

Do I gotta crack a vertebrae
To get a point across
Of a rap holocaust
Will pipes exhaust
Peeps dead in streets
One who told me
You gotta make em' feel you
When you ride on a beat
Cool attitude
Ready for the heat
More that I speak
See all eyes on Tee
Bloodline traced back
2 Kings and Queens
Slaves became men
We can do anything
Pull up your pants
Strap up your boots
Watch 5 o'clock news
Then sit and watch Roots

I love you brother
Now Nigga I shoot
We all love
Kicks, chicks, money and hoop
Stay on the low
Only let you know
Live with the band
Or I'm gonna do a show
Call me tee will
The new Negro.
My vision board
Three comma dough

18. Holding On Verse 2.5

Think of all things
You're grateful for
Know all things
That you really want to do
MadLove told me
So I'm a tell you
Change is a must
Striving for balance
Seek and conquer
Any given challenge
Some say it's luck
But I say it's talent
Clouds go away
Souls get strong
Find a purpose
So name lives on
Wealth is long
Climb and lift
Help the ones
You used to run with

When my shadows gone
Footprints will be there
In a world so cold
Be the one that's rare
Draw out dreams
Watch em' unfold
Manifest magic
When actions are gold
Hard when you try
2 do it all on your own
Dad said boy you understand
When you get grown

19. Love's L.A.W. Hook

Pinch ya' on the cheek

Give your forehead a kiss

Didn't think I could love

Someone like this

Everything that I dream

You are the purpose

We're always connected

Just like cursive

20. Love's L.A.W. Verse 1

Fall asleep on my heart
That's your #1 place
1st thing in the morning
Put a smile on my face
Walking in the kitchen
And you're wrapped around my leg
Sitting on my shoulders
Baby duck your head
Waking up to go Pee
Would always let me know
Cherish every moment
Watching my baby grow
Pampers turned to pull ups
Now you're wearing draws
Dad their panties, I sigh and pause
Turn down my help
When I buckle you in
Tell me "I got it",
When tying up your shoes
Footprints on the Mirror

After your bath
Say "dad your funny ",
When I make you laugh
Chasing after bubbles
Life is fun
In a big field
Playing tag and run
My hand was your pillow
In your car seat
Drove around the neighborhood
Until you fell asleep
At the dinner table
Feet not touching the floor
Holding my hand
Walking up to the store
Riding in the grocery cart
Cute as can be
Burping in my ear
Would give me relief
Hiding under pillows
Camouflaged in
One day I couldn't find ya'
Blended rite in
Reason for my being
Spark to my soul
Yourd hugs warm my heart
I ain't ever letting go!!

21. Love's L.A.W. Verse 2

Fart bubbles in the bath
Playing with a billion toys
In Jiu Jitsu class
Tapping out older boys
All your baby teeth
Falling outta your mouth
My little sugar cup
Girl raised in the south
Prayed you would sneeze
Cuzz ya couldn't blow your nose
Chased me in the yard
Laughing with the water hose
Pretend I'm your horse
Or a big Dog
Riding on my back
Hoping you don't fall
You took your 1st step
My heart skipped a beat
Holding my breath
As you walked to me

I couldn't clip your nails
Scared to hurt my baby
Time to go to bed
Now you acting all crazy
First time you rolled over
Was like a touchdown
Daddy daughter dates
Ice cream downtown
Beat box on your belly
Laugh you to sleep
Don't wanna wake you up
So I creep, creep, creep

www.ingramcontent.com/pod-product-compliance
Lightning Source LLC
LaVergne TN
LVHW051239200726
843510LV00011B/1613